Table of Contents

About the Author

Victor is a Real Estate Investor, Developer & Investment Manager born in Lagos Nigeria, based in Atlanta Ga USA who started out his investing career in 2012. He obtained his Bachelors of Business Administration degree in Finance and is the Founder of conglomerate firm Zirowin Group. Our portfolio includes Zirow Invest LLC, Zirowin Capital (Real Estate Development & Investment Management), OFFERVEST (Home Buying Firm).

Collectively his business portfolio has acquired and closed over $4M dollars worth over real estate & been a keystone in closing 50+ investment deals with investors. He has been featured in notable publications such as Forbes Magazine, Black Enterprise & was nominated for Rice Awards business person of the year in 2018. His group of companies specializes in the acquisitions, financial analysis, development, and reselling of residential and commercial investment properties. He also has extensive experience working with investors of all ranges (domestic & international) from new investors, all the way up to multi-million dollar private equity hedge funds. The asset types he specializes in are Single Family Homes, Land, & Multifamily properties. He values building relationships and doing business with integrity, while executing and closing deals on a very high level.

His personal mission statement is: to be an inspiration to the world, to empower people to pursue their passions, embrace their journey, and follow their dreams.

Victor E. Bomi

Introduction

Being an immigrant in America, and having been able to build a successful business here, I have seen first hand how much opportunity there is to do well and thrive, in any industry - as long as you apply yourself. The real estate industry here is no different and since 2012 I have had the opportunity to work with investors from all over the world, including Hong Kong, Australia, Isreal, West Africa, and London. The American market is a stable market and still ripe for more Foreign Direct Investment.

By the end of this book, if you are a foreign national who is ready to take the dive into the American real estate market, you will have the know how to do so. Thank you for your support & enjoy the second edition of Investing In American Real Estate + (International Investor)

PURPOSE: The overall purpose of this book is to provide prospective international investors who would like to invest in American Real Estate the necessary foundation to get started.

WHO THIS BOOK IS FOR: This book is for investors who are looking to create financial security through real estate investing, build upon already established wealth, and for international investors who are interested in acquiring investment properties in America.

WHY YOU SHOULD INVEST IN REAL ESTATE: Historically, real estate investing has created the most millionaires in the world out of any asset class and is the #1 way to achieve financial freedom to provide a legacy & peace of mind for your loved ones.

Introduction to Investment In America

The size of the Global Real Estate market in totality is around $217 Trillion **(the size of just the American market is $33 Trillion**, which makes up roughly 15% of the entire real estate market in the world. With this sheer size of the American market comes a subset of opportunities for foreign real estate investors to put their capital to work into profitable market opportunities in America, both in the commercial and residential sectors. It is a secure way to protect your wealth, and create even more, with the right investment plan.

Social Stability

Liquidity (easier to buy and sell properties)

Secure Political System

Portfolio & Currency Diversification

Clear Land Ownership Rights

Transparent Transaction System

Great Financing System for Investors

It Is A Buyers Market (Better Deals For You)

In the last few weeks, foreign investors have been investing heavily in America real estate as a hedge against the coronavirus - as they see the US Market as a safe-haven, hedge against the pandemic's market risk **(Source: CNBC)**

$78 - Billion
(USA Foreign Direct Investments in 2019)

Understanding The Market

Key Legal Terms To Know

The legal name for a foreign investor/person investing in the United States is called an **(NRA) Non-Resident Alien** & the legal term for your investment in the United States is called a **United States Real Property Interest (USRPI)** An interest in real property located in the United States or the Virgin Islands. The definition of USRPI includes any interest, except an interest solely as a creditor. USRPI also includes associated personal property. Review (Internal Revenue Code 897 - to get a better understanding of USRPI) - https://www.irs.gov/irm/part4/irm_04-061-012)

The price ranges for investment properties will vary depending on the market you choose to invest in.

the average price per sq.ft for American homes is $123/sq.ft.

Current Median Home Values (Key Markets)

ATLANTA, GEORGIA - $299,308

LOS ANGELES, CALIFORNIA - $752,508

AUSTIN, TEXAS - $401,999

TAMPA, FLORIDA - $251,387

MANHATTAN, NEW YORK - $998,557

Preliminary Steps to Take Before Investing

Top Factors To Consider Before Buying A Property In A Particular Market

GDP, Industries In Market, Population Size & Growth Rate, Jobs Available & Median Income, School Districts Ratings, Supply and Demand, Average Days on Market for Properties for Sale, Crime Rate, Condition of Property Itself, Price & Discount to Retail Rate, The Current Economic Phase of the American Real Estate Market, (The Location) Property Proximity to - entertainment, airports, hotels, and hospitals

Key Questions You Should Ask Yourself Before Embarking Into A New Market In America

How will you be financing your investments?

How much is your total investment budget?

What type of properties are you interested in?

What is your risk tolerance? (aggressive or conservative)

What is your investment goal? Capital Gains or Consistent Monthly Cashflow?

How many properties do you intend on acquiring in a given time period?

Do you have resources, teams, and experienced contacts in the market you are targeting?

Do you have the correct entity for investing in America (for both legal & tax purposes?)

Financing Your Investments In the USA

You wouldn't meet the general lending guidelines to qualify for the traditional mortgage (which include)

→ CREDIT SCORE

→ CREDIT HISTORY

→ VERIFIABLE INCOME (W2s & Tax Returns)

→ VERIFIABLE DOWN-PAYMENT

→ SOURCE OF FUNDS

→ AMERICAN BANK & BANK STATEMENTS

The system for financing real estate in America is great for its citizens but a bit more stringent for foreign investors who are not all-cash buyers. The reason behind this is that most bank lenders are wary of lending to people outside their home country - as the risk is deemed much too high to bear.

The largest lenders in the USA are Fannie Mae & Freddie Mac (who do not lend to foreign investors) and because that's who finances most of the home loans in the country (their criteria is the industry standard and what a lot of banks use as their own lending guidelines) If you are here on a green card or a work visa, then that's a loophole and work around that would benefit for you as both Freddie Mac and Fannie Mae will finance you.

Financing Your Investments In the USA

What To Do About Financing Restrictions

Global Banks Who Finance International Investors

You will likely have to apply for a Foreign National Mortgage Loan (be sure to have all your financial documents in place and ready)

Apply with an international **(global) bank** that operates offices in your home country & the US

Citi Bank

HSBC

BBVA

Compass

1st Capital Group

Quontic Bank

Portfolio Lenders

Another option is to secure financing through **a portfolio lender** (these lenders hold their mortgages in a portfolio of loans, and generally have a less strict qualification criteria since they are not re-selling their mortgages in the secondary market to Fannie, Freddie, and VA)

Financing Your Investments In the USA

Applying For A Foreign National Loan (Documents You Need)

Visa/Passport of the country you are a legal citizen of (make sure all your paperwork is up to date)

proof of income in the form of bank statements (will usually require the last 1-2 years)

proof of employment (reference letter from your current employer)

a credit reference in your home country (from a financial institution that has lent you money)

credit card statements over the last 12 months (to know what your borrowing habits are)

Financing Your Investments In the USA

The Costs Of Your Loan

CLOSING COSTS

INSURANCE

FLOOD CERTIFICATIONS

LOAN ORIGINATION FEES

PRE-PAID INTEREST

Key Financing Points To Know

You can **expect higher rates** as a non-citizen, You will have to put down **a larger down-payment** (the average down-payment required for a first time home buyer that is a citizen in 2018, was 7% according to a survey by the National Association of Realtors) - compared to usually a **20-50% down payment** requirement to you just because you are a foreign investor, your funds for your down-payment need to be "seasoned" in an American account for at least 30-60 days

"Cash Is King! A lot of the hurdles mentioned earlier can simply be avoided if you are an all cash buyer, the process will generally be a lot faster and less complicated for you."

Loan Types To Note

Adjustable Rate

Fixed Rate

Interest Only

Loan Terms: Most conventional loans range from 15-30 years, while most hard money loans are usually short term 6-12 month loans

Property Acquisitions

Key Team Members You Need

Power of Attorney (who can act on your behalf here & sign any required documents and contracts)

Mortgage broker (if you need financing)

Investment Manager (to secure good deals & manage the entire investment process (acquisitions, construction, dispositions - from start to finish)

International Attorney (entity structuring)

CPA (tax positioning & protection)

Property Management Company (asset management

Language Translator Service (to translate your documents to English (if you are not proficient in English)

Agent (to list & resell your properties)

Finding Properties (On Market vs. Off Market)

Properties in the United States can be bought "On Market" through a listing portal called the **Multiple Listing Service (MLS)** via a real estate agent (usually priced at retail and in bidding wars with other aggressive buyers) or **Off-Market via private sellers and wholesalers** (you are likely to get a better deal)

At (ZI) We specialize in sourcing off-market and direct to seller - discounted deals to our investor clients.

Property Acquisitions (Time To Buy Your Property)

NEED TO KNOWS

Before closing on a property here are a few things you need to have researched and done your due diligence on:

are you getting a good deal?

If the property is vacant or rented?

if rented for how much? whats the gross income?

what the operating expenses are? the net income?

if it needs any repairs, if so what needs updating?

what zip code & county is it located in?
(is it considered a desirable location?)

what are homes in the area already selling for?

what the market rents are?

insurance costs?

management fees?

the school district ratings?

Communication is Key

Staying in **consistent contact** with all parties involved with the transaction (seller, agent, closing agent, power of attorney, investment manager & anyone else involved) to keep everyone on the same page is very important to having a successful closing - you need to know exactly what is going on and don't make any assumptions that everyone is on the same page.

BONUS TIP: You also need to know upfront that you will be paying property taxes when you acquire the property. These are taxes you pay to the local state & county in which your property is located in, based on the % assessed value of the property (it will vary from state to state, county to county)

(these taxes are different from the income & capital gains taxes - which we discuss later on in the book)

Property Acquisitions (Miscellaneous)

OPERATIONAL COSTS TO BE PREPARED FOR

Legal Fees

CPA and Accountant Fees

Investment Management Fees

Property Management Fees

Insurance Costs

Property Maintenance Costs

Mortgage & Interest Costs (if you take out a loan)

VISA & Travel Costs (if you are determined to come to the states, will need arrangements to get your US Visa, air-fair, hotel & lodging, etc)

Operational Resources You Need

US Virtual Mail Service & Address
Service Providers: Earth Class Mail, Anytime Mailbox, Traveling Mailbox, iPostal1

US Based Phone Number
Service Providers: Google Voice, Dingtone, Telzio, FreedomPop, Voiceably

Property Acquisitions (Miscellaneous)

LEGAL ENTITY & FORMATION STRUCTURE

You can buy in your personal name

A Trust - fiduciary arrangement, allows 3rd party / trustee to hold assets on behalf of beneficiaries

Ownership via (FC) Foreign Corporation

Ownership through a US Company - that is Owned by A FC

Ownership through a Limited Partnership (LP),

Ownership through a Limited Liability Company (LLC)

(There are many more ways to structure your entity)

This is a critical step, that you should take very seriously because of the tax implications. At (ZI) we can help you find a good CPA that will structure your legal entity for you, just note that there is no perfect solution - as every entity has its pros and cons. Ultimately your goals and unique situation should determine how you structure your buying entity.

TAXES 101 (Navigating Tax Laws)

As a foreign investor buying property in the US, the key component that will affect your tax implications will be how you structure the ownership of the property.

When Deciding Ownership Structure

Ask: am I purchasing to resell?

to hold as rental income?

what is my hold period?

do I intend to pass it off to heirs?

or for personal use? if personal use - by who?

Individual Tax Identification Number (ITIN):
The IRS issues this # to foreign nationals for the purpose of filing your federal taxes since you are not eligible for a social security #

(a good **CPA** can help you set this up)

Key Tax Rules: Foreign Investment In Real Property Tax Act (FIRPTA)

This is a form of capital gains tax **Withholding Tax** - when you want to sell a property as a foreign investor this is the tax you will pay (the Internal Revenue Service) will withhold **between 10-15% of the gross sales price** of the property.

In the transaction, the buyer actually acts as the Withholding Agent and is responsible to do the with-holding to send the required withholding amount (as of today max cap of 15% of sales price) to the IRS. (when closing an international deal - your closing attorney/title company should be well versed on these rules and regulations)

Bonus Tip: To properly execute and comply with the laws of the with-holding tax - be sure that you have an **ITIN #** registered

Withholding Tax Exemptions

a. Sales Price Under $300k

b. The buyer is an individual and not a corporate entity

c. The buyer will use the property as his or her residence for at least 50% of the year for the first 2 years of ownership

d. if you're not considered a foreign individual or a withholding certificate

TAXES 101 (Navigating Tax Laws)

Key Tax Rules: Estate / Inheritance Tax (when you pass)

If you were to pass away, you are giving an exemption of $60,000 against the value of your asset in the taxable estate, but anything over this $60,000 is taxed (the usual estate tax rate is 16% (and federal transfer tax, can be up to 40%) can avoid this tax by investing & acquiring the property via a foreign entity - but there are pros and cons to this as well.

(consult tax and legal advisors)

TAXES 101 (Navigating Tax Laws)

Key Tax Rules: Income Tax (during hold period)

NRAs, are required to pay US income taxes on any income in/from the USA. Rental income on your investment will be subjected to a **30% flat withholding tax** (unless your home country has an income tax treaty with the USA, that would reduce it to the 10-15% range)

(deprecation and operating expenses can be used as a tax shield - your CPA will advise you on how to do this) (this should be planned separately from those laws affecting estate taxes as they are different laws)

TAXES 101 (Navigating Tax Laws)

Key Tax Rules: Tax Cuts and Jobs Act (TCJA)

a windfall that benefits both foreign and domestic investors, **the corporate tax rate has been dropped from 35% to 21%,** which essentially makes it more attractive to acquire your properties in an American corporation as opposed to a trust or individual type of ownership structure when acquiring your properties) (This is much lower than the gains for individual and trust income which is still taxed at 37%)

TAXES 101 (Navigating Tax Laws)

TAX TREATIES

Countries around the world have agreed to tax treaties with the United States, these treaties are beneficial to you as a foreign investor - and greatly reduces your taxes or even be exempt in certain cases - you can find out if your country has a treaty with America & learn more about them here: https://www.irs.gov/businesses/international-businesses/united-states-income-tax-treaties-a-to-z

EB-5 VISA PROGRAM

"The Quickest Way to Get A Green Card in the USA" - FORBES MAGAZINE 2016

This references the **Employment-Based Immigration, Fifth Preference Investor Program** and overseen by the United States Citizenship and Immigration Services **(USCIS).**

This program (subject to meeting capital investment amount requirements & job creation requirements) grants immigrant entrepreneurs and their spouses + unmarried children under 21 a permanent residency green card.

EB-5 VISA PROGRAM

QUALIFICATION CRITERIA FOR EB5 VISA PROGRAM

i. Investing in a commercial (for-profit) enterprise in the US
ii. Creating or preserving 10 permanent full-time jobs for qualified US employees

CAPITAL INVESTMENT REQUIREMENT FOR EB5 VISA PROGRAM

Applicants must invest $900,000 or $1,800,000 into a US commercial enterprise (if the commercial enterprise is based in a Target Employment Area (TEA) then the minimum amount the investor needs to invest is only $900,000.

(To qualify for the USCIS TEA Designation, the investment must be located in high unemployment and rural locations)

E2 TREATY VISA PROGRAM

Allows an immigrant of a treaty country (country in which US maintains treaties of commerce and navigation) to enter and work inside the US based on an investment he or she will be controlling while inside the US

CAPITAL INVESTMENT REQUIREMENT FOR E2 VISA PROGRAM

(Minimum of $100,000 investment Required)

CONCLUSION

KEY TAKEAWAYS: You have to be able to move quickly (have all your ducks in a row), usually investment deals are first come first serve here, and usually go to the investor that is most prepared + ready to execute quickly

KEY MISTAKES TO AVOID

Not properly setting up your investment entity with a legal professional, not having your financing structure in place prior to looking to invest, not having a specific idea of what type of investment strategy you are most interested in (cash flow or capital gains), investing in a market that you haven't done your due diligence on, not working with an experienced investment professional in the market you are investing in

RESOURCES FOR YOU

1. PDF Guide for Foreign Investment Taxation, by top us CPA Firm Deloitte
2. Purchasing Real Estate In US via Anderson Tax LLC
3. Action Steps for International Investor by Zirow Invest

VISIT -zirowinvest.com/resources

I would like to hear your feedback on the book.
(email: info@victorbomi.com or dm me on Instagram @VictorBomi)

THANK YOU

Thank you for reading Investing In American Real Estate + International Investor. I enjoy connecting with and building relationships with people from all over the world, learning and experiencing different cultures, and sharing my culture with others as well - all while being able to close on amazing real estate investment deals at (ZI). It has been a pleasure to write this edition of Investing In American Real Estate+. If you are an international investor who is serious about investing in the American market, don't hesitate to visit our website and schedule a free consultation zirowinvest.com/consultation
(or email us your inquiry at info@zirowin.com)

Share this book with a friend or 2 who will find value in it.

I wish you continued blessings, and cheers to your success.

-Victor E. Bomi, CEO Zirow Invest, LLC.

REFERENCES

https://www.investopedia.com/articles/mortages-real_estate/11/factors-affecting-real-estate-market.asp

https://www.irs.gov/irm/part4/irm_04-061-012

https://www.irs.gov/individuals/international-taxpayers/firpta-withholding

https://taxsummaries.pwc.com/united-states/corporat

https://www.thetaxadviser.com/issues/2018/sep/restructuring-foreign-investment-us-real-property.html

https://www.uscis.gov/eb-5

https://www.irs.gov/businesses/small-businesses-self-employed/tips-on-rental-real-estate-income-deductions-and-recordkeeping

https://www.eb5diligence.com/articles/eb-5-visa-requirements

https://www.manhattanmiami.com/can-foreigners-buy-property-in-the-usa

https://myrawealth.com/insights/can-a-foreigner-buy-a-house-in-the-us

https://en.wikipedia.org/wiki/Foreign_investment_in_United_States_real_estate

https://www.zillow.com/research/california-leads-housing-gains-22600/

https://www.thebalance.com/u-s-gdp-current-statistics-3305731

https://www.nerdwallet.com/article/mortgages/the-20-mortgage-down-payment-is-dead

https://www.bpbcpa.com/considerations-for-foreign-investors-in-u-s-real-estate-after-u-s-tax-reform-by-ken-vitek-cpa/

https://markjkohler.com/rules-for-foreigners-investing-in-rental-property-in-the-u-s/

https://sftaxcounsel.com/practice-areas/international-tax-attorneys/u-s-tax-planning-for-foreigners-intending-to-own-u-s-real-estate/

https://www.fool.com/millionacres/taxes/depreciation/real-estate-101-rental-property-depreciation-rules-all-investors-should-know/